IMAGES
of America

BEDMINSTER

This photograph was taken at the dividing line between the old and the new Bedminster. The Essex Hounds travel down Burnt Mills Road, leaving a quiet little farm in their dust. Perhaps no one knew that sleepy Sunday morning in 1900 that the days of the family farm were numbered. Surely no one expected that within 30 years, all the farms would be gone, transformed into great estates. (James S. Jones.)

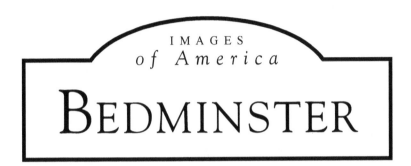

IMAGES
of America

BEDMINSTER

William A. Schleicher and Amanda R. Schleicher

ARCADIA
PUBLISHING

Published by Arcadia Publishing
Charleston, South Carolina

Library of Congress Catalog Card Number: 98-88257

For all general information contact Arcadia Publishing at:
Telephone 843-853-2070
Fax 843-853-0044
E-mail sales@arcadiapublishing.com
For customer service and orders:
Toll-Free 1-888-313-2665

Visit us on the Internet at www.arcadiapublishing.com

CONTENTS

ACKNOWLEDGMENTS

To the many people who shared their treasured photographs and stories with us, we extend our heartfelt thanks: Mike Deak; Dean Durling; Janet Castelpietra; Tom D'Amico; Steve Forbes; Oliver D. Filley; Pamela Hill; T. Leonard Hill; James S. Jones; Mrs. Screven Lorillard; Kenneth B. Schley Jr.; Dorothy Stratford; and Jack Turpin.

We would also like to thank the following organizations for giving us access to their archives: The Branchburg Historical Society; The Clarence Dillon Memorial Library; The Masters of the Essex Foxhounds; The Peapack Gladstone Cultural and Heritage Commission; The Peapack Gladstone Library; the Rutgers University Alexander Library Special Collection; Princeton University; The Somerset County Historical Society, The Somerset County Library; The Somerset County Planning Board; *The Somerset Messenger Gazette*; and the United States Equestrian Team.

Please note that the names in parentheses at the end of each caption indicate the source of the photograph, not the source of the information for the caption. All photographs credited to E. Van Doren were printed by the authors from glass negatives originally made by local photographer Edythe Van Doren about the turn of the century. We are indebted to the Peapack Gladstone Cultural and Heritage Commission for access to, and permission to use, these negatives. In return, all the prints made from the Van Doren collection, including many not used in this work, will be given to the Peapack Gladstone Cultural and Heritage Commission upon completion of the project. The authors would also like to thank Mr. and Mrs. William Hayes for the use of their darkroom and photographic equipment.

INTRODUCTION

At the turn of the century, a young lady named Edythe (Lane) Van Doren purchased an Ascot number 41 bellows camera and went into the photography business. Her two product lines were postcards and portraits. Over the next 20 years, she produced hundreds of photographs from four-by-five-inch glass negatives. Virtually all of them were what we would today call time exposures, being exposed from several seconds to two or three minutes. Naturally some of the subjects, especially the animals, were unable to sit still for that long. In some pictures, you will see people resting their heads on their hands to keep from moving.

As Mrs. Van Doren traveled around town, recording everything she saw, she must not have realized that she was capturing on film the end of an era. For two hundred years, Bedminster had been a sleepy little farm community. In many ways, it had been a place of refuge. It served as such for Daniel Axtell, son of the regicide, who had been one of those responsible for the beheading of King Charles I, and who had in turn been condemned to death upon accession to the throne of the King's son, Charles II. It was a place of refuge for Palatine German allies of England who had been dispossessed by the depredations of the Thirty Years War and the War of Grand Alliance. It was while finding refuge in Bedminster during the American Revolution, that a patriot family gave birth in Lamington to Zebulon Pike, the famous general and explorer.

During the American Revolution, the farms and hamlets of Bedminster witnessed much activity on the part of the American army, and occasional intrusions by the enemy. General Knox established his Artillery Park, our nation's first military academy, where the Hills development now stands. It was there that a grand ball and fete was held to honor the French ambassador, and the minister of the governor of Havana, on behalf of the King of Spain. The murder of Miss Jane McCreain, daughter of the minister of the Lamington church, in what is now upstate New York by Native Americans associated with the British, undermined support for Burgoyne among settlers of that region and contributed to his defeat. Until the end of the last century, this incident was considered too important to be left out of any history of the American Revolution.

From the time the last cannon was fired at the Artillery Park until the early part of this century, when Edythe Van Doren was recording everything she saw, Bedminster reverted into a bucolic farming community centered around village churches. But even as Mrs. Van Doren was freezing its history on glass plates, the seeds of change had already been sown. During the 1890s, wealthy New Yorkers began to establish country estates in the Bernardsville "Mountain

Colony." There being no more available land in Bernardsville, the sons and daughters of those who had settled there, as well as new arrivals, began to establish estates in Far Hills, Peapack, and Gladstone. In 1890, Grant Schley had the railroad extended to those three hamlets. In that same year, Charles Pfizer bought a 200-acre farm in Gladstone (at that time, Peapack and Gladstone were still part of Bedminster) and made it the seat of the Essex Hounds.

With permission of the farmers, the Essex Hounds with their owner, Charles Pfizer, and his guests, hunted foxes on the farms of Bedminster and the surrounding area. The third generation of the original Bernardsville Mountain Colony settlers began to buy those farms. Sometimes the farmer who had sold his land was hired-on to work the land as a tenant farmer for the new owner. By the 1930s, Bedminster had been completely transformed from family farms to estates of the landed gentry. In most, if not all cases, this represented an economic benefit to the farmers, who enjoyed a more reliable income and a better standard of living. During the Depression, many of the farmers and local tradesmen were provided much needed employment on the great estates.

The first six chapters of this book present a view of life in rural Bedminster at the turn of the century. You may be surprised to learn that there was a casino in Pluckemin at that time, or that sleepy little Pottersville was a center of industry. It may dismay you to see some of the important Revolutionary War sites that have been lost. If you like railroads, you'll love the "Rockabye Baby" (Rockaway Valley) Rail Way that flourished during this period, and then disappeared about the same time as the family farm.

The seventh chapter shows what Bedminster became over the period from the 1890s to the 1930s, and largely what it is today. Wall to wall, Bedminster provides a hospitable refuge for the landed gentry. The Essex Foxhounds still run twice a week, and the United States Equestrian Team has made its home here in the nation's most exclusive horse country. Many of the descendants of the original estate owners still live here. Occasionally a worthy newcomer will find an available property. Malcolm Forbes brought his family here in 1947, and his sons Steve and Christopher (Kip) still make Bedminster their home. Enjoy this peek at one of the most interesting communities in the nation.

One

PLUCKEMIN

On a warm, lazy summer afternoon in 1900, photographer Edythe Van Doren captured this image of the village of Pluckemin from the Burnt Mills Road. (E. Van Doren.)

Following his stunning victories at Trenton and Princeton, which turned the tide of the war in his favor, George Washington stayed here Saturday and Sunday, January 4 and 5, 1777, on his way to the winter encampment in Morristown. The house was built about 1750, and was demolished in the 1940s. (E. Van Doren.)

The Jacobus Vanderveer house just north of town was headquarters to General Knox during the Middlebrook encampment of 1778–79. Knox established an artillery school where the Hills development is today. That school was the precursor of West Point. The house is currently being restored to become a museum. (Somerset County Library.)

The Bedminster Dutch Reformed Church was originally located just north of the Vanderveer house, where the cemetery is today. Although Jacob Vanderveer was an elder in the church and had donated the land for the cemetery, he was unable to have General Knox's infant daughter (who was not yet baptized) or his own daughter (who was insane) buried there. (Rutgers Special Collection.)

This view of the interior of the Bedminster Reformed Church was taken about 1880, as was the previous photograph. The church was later demolished and replaced by a much bigger building, which is still located on Route 202 in Bedminster Village (see p. 40). (Rutgers Special Collection.)

The "Top Notch Lodge," which still stands on the hill overlooking Route 202/206 south of Pluckemin, was the headquarters for the Ku Klux Klan in the early part of the century. This photograph was taken about 1915. (Rutgers Special Collection.)

"The Yellow Lantern" tearoom was built by Fred Eick on land purchased from the Wyckoff family. Fred and his wife, Hilda, lived there. This photograph was taken in 1926. The building was demolished in 1974. (Clarence Dillon Memorial Library.)

With Pluckemin in the background, the Peapack Stagecoach lumbers down the road to Somerville. The stagecoach made the run between Peapack and Somerville until about 1912. (E. Van Doren.)

"Elm Cottage" was located on the west side of Route 202/206, south of the Burnt Mills Road intersection. It was taken down by City Federal Savings Bank in 1980. (E. Van Doren.)

The Pluckemin Store was moved diagonally across the intersection to its present location after the original store burned in 1892. This photograph was taken about 1902. (E. Van Doren.)

The Peapack Stagecoach is making its mid-day stop in front of the Pluckemin General Store about 1902. You can see driver Charlie Wikoff's hands holding the reins as he sits in a compartment in the front of the coach. All of Edythe Van Doren's photographs were time exposures, which explains the white horse's double ear and the ghost of the man who walked around the back of the coach while the photograph was being exposed. (E. Van Doren.)

14

The sign on the Pluckemin Store reads "Raritan ABC Paints, Best on Earth, Raritan Paint Mill, Raritan N.J." Another sign advertises Syracuse Plows. The post office was located in the store. (E. Van Doren.)

This shed, behind the Pluckemin Store, was called affectionately "Charley's home." Sausage was ground in these buildings in a grinder powered by a horse on a treadle. (E. Van Doren.)

Here is the corner of Main Street (now Route 202/206) looking down Mountain Avenue (Washington Valley Road) about 1902. The Kenilworth Inn is on the left. (E. Van Doren.)

Known as the "Queen Ann Cottage" in 1904, this house was later a barbershop, a candy store, and other kinds of businesses before being demolished to make way for a gas station. (E. Van Doren.)

The "Mountain View Farm" house, formally located just north of Route 78 on the west side of Routes 202/206, was taken down by City Federal Savings Bank in 1980. At the time that this photograph was taken, about 1903, it was Will Powelson's house. (E. Van Doren.)

The Mary Voorhees house, photographed in 1902, was located on Main Street in Pluckemin. (E. Van Doren.)

The Kenilworth Inn opened in 1899 on the site of Eoff's Revolutionary War-era tavern. The inn had 20 bedrooms at $3 per day or $12–18 per week. After the inn failed it was used for awhile as the state police barracks. It burned down in 1928. The Pluckemin shopping center with the A&P is now located on this site. (E. Van Doren.)

This is the dining room in the Kenilworth Inn. The photograph was taken during the summer of 1901. (E. Van Doren.)

18

This combined coach barn and stable, photographed in the winter of 1900, served the needs of the Kenilworth Inn and its patrons. (E. Van Doren.)

The inn boasted a casino and a nine-hole golf course. Although gambling was permitted, the hotel was on the temperance plan. Water served in the dining room and sold by the bottle came from the Culm Rock Springs, about a mile from the property. (E. Van Doren.)

In 1852, the Dutch Reformed Church built this Greek Revival chapel in Pluckemin. The building was later converted to a grocery store by John L. Dolliver. About the turn of the century, when this photograph was taken, the store was operated by Asher Smith. It was later abandoned and then renovated by Fred Walter to become the home that can still be seen on Main Street. (E. Van Doren.)

In this detail of the above photograph, Asher Smith can be seen on the porch. (E. Van Doren.)

This is Mr. Asher Smith in his road wagon about 1903. (E. Van Doren.)

This portrait of four generations in the Smith family was taken in the photographer's yard. (E. Van Doren.)

This house on Burnt Mills Road is known as the Gaston house. It was sold by Robert Gaston to John Wickenhaver in 1886. His son, George, bought the house from his estate in 1914, and sold it to Aaron and Florence Wickenhaver Johnson in 1942. (E. Van Doren.)

In 1900, at the dawn of the automobile age, all the roads were narrow and unpaved. Dust was a problem when it was dry, and when it rained the roads turned to mud. (E. Van Doren.)

"The Lyon's Den" was built about 1890 by Adrian Lyon as a home for his father. (E. Van Doren.)

Here is another view of Main Street (now Route 202/206), at the north end of town, taken about 1902. (E. Van Doren.)

Pluckamin Church, Pluckamin, N. J.

Here is the Pluckemin Presbyterian Church, as it appeared during the winter of 1900–1901. (Branchburg Historical Society.)

This view of the interior of the Pluckemin Presbyterian Church was taken in 1900 (E. Van Doren.)

The streetscape from the front of the church no longer appears as it did in 1965. Historic structures were removed to provide access to the Pluckemin Park adult living center. (Rutgers Special Collection.)

At Thanksgiving in 1906, the church was decorated from God's bountiful harvest. (E. Van Doren.)

The Pluckemin Presbyterian Church Parsonage in 1902 was the fifth house north of the church on Main Street. (E. Van Doren.)

This is a view of the interior of the Pluckemin Presbyterian Church Parsonage as it appeared about 1900. (E. Van Doren.)

The Pluckemin Schoolhouse in 1902 had been built as a Methodist chapel in 1831. It was originally located where the church parking lot is now, and moved to its present site in 1858. It served as Pluckemin's school until the brick schoolhouse on Burnt Mills Road was completed in 1912. (E. Van Doren.)

These members of the Pluckemin School Class of 1905, listed from left to right, are as follows: (bottom row) three unidentified, Ruth Voorhees, Addie Robinson, two unidentified, Alfred Burd, and unidentified; (middle row) two unidentified, J. Harold Tefyel, unidentified, Marshall Woods, Edna Dmorapart, unidentified, Roy Barken (baby), Elsie Compton, and Newton Burd; (top row) Ala Hodget, unidentified, Lizzie Smith, Amy Hodget, Eve Wickenhaver, unidentified, Millie Compton, Silis Watski, ? Burd, and Tirtruda Loed. (E. Van Doren.)

This view of Miss Alice Lyon's house on Main Street was taken about 1900. The house was built in 1850. Today it houses the offices of Caldwell Banker Real Estate. (E. Van Doren.)

Miss Lyon kept a carpenter busy for years making alterations and additions to the house. The carriage house at the rear of the property was built for Miss Lyon's automobiles about 1910. This tree house outside the Lyon house was constructed in the spring of 1901. The photographer, Edythe Van Doren, found it to be a good subject for a postcard. (E. Van Doren.)

28

Charlie Lyon is seated at the tiller of his 1903 curved dash Oldsmobile in the side yard of the Lyon house. (E. Van Doren.)

Miss Lyon was famous for her automobiles. Here she is in the front seat of her 1905 touring car, with Charlie in a chauffeur's outfit posing with one foot on the running board. (E. Van Doren.)

Here is Mrs. Lyon's 1906 16-horsepower Compound touring car. Manufactured in New Jersey by the Eisenhuth Horseless Vehicle Company, the Compound used a Graham-Fox 3-cylinder engine in which the center cylinder was powered solely by exhaust gasses from the other two cylinders. The engine was reputed to be very smooth running and silent. (E. Van Doren.)

Called "Hillside," the Coriell house was located where the Hills development is today. This photograph was taken about 1904. (E. Van Doren.)

Known as "The Maples," this house belonged to William Compton at the turn of the century and was later owned by his son Anson. More recently, the property belonged to John Harrison, who had a chicken farm and marketed his chickens in Newark. (E. Van Doren.)

This farm was called the "Washington Park Farm" because it was the site of an artillery camp in 1778–79. It is now the location of the Hills development. (E. Van Doren.)

31

The Pluckemin Woolen Mills, also known as the Somerville Woolen Mills, was built in 1895 on the south side of Chambers Brook, below the milldam. From 1905 to 1910, the name was changed to the Somerville Manufacturing Company. In 1911 the Superior Thread and Yarn Company purchased the property. It was demolished in 1927. (E. Van Doren.)

At the time that this photograph was taken, in 1902, the woolen mill was known locally as Brown's mill, since it had been founded by James Brown Jr. (E. Van Doren.)

The old log mill dam was located at the west end of Echo Lake. (E. Van Doren.)

This photograph shows the location of the mill, in relation to the dam on the left. In 1924, the mill was sold to the Somerset Aniline Works, which made dyes from coaltar. Unfortunately, the ground could not absorb the dye residue, and it escaped into the stream. They eventually closed down at the request of the Fish and Game Division. (E. Van Doren.)

Here are the members of the Pluckemin Base Ball Club, photographed on the steps of the Kenilworth Inn in 1902. (E. Van Doren.)

Echo Lake makes a romantic spot for a moonlight stroll, and was a good subject for a postcard. (E. Van Doren.)

Two

BEDMINSTER VILLAGE

This picture, simply entitled "Elwood's Horse," was taken in the summer of 1900. At that time, Bedminster Village was known as Lesser Cross Roads. (E. Van Doren.)

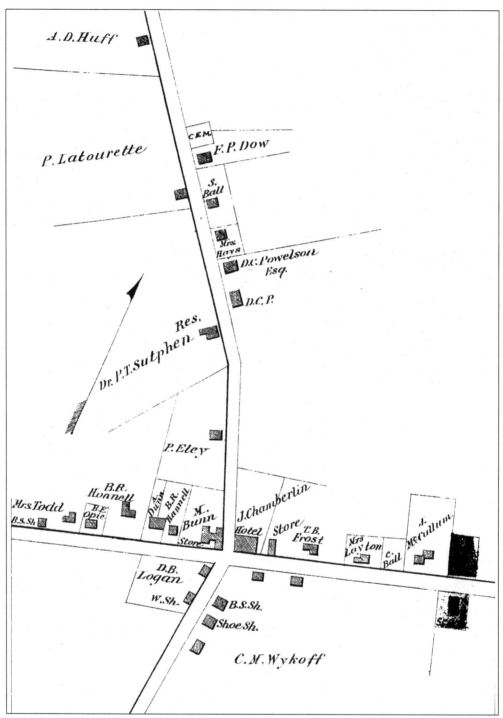

This map of Lesser Cross Roads appeared in the 1873 Beers Atlas.

In 1786 Aaron Mellick built the original part of the Bedminster Inn for his son John. Pres. Woodrow Wilson delivered a campaign speech here in 1916. It has been in continuous operation for over two hundred years. Today it is called "Willie's Tavern." (Rutgers Special Collection.)

The 235-acre Nevius homestead on Somerville Road was built in 1772. Until 1971, seven consecutive generations of the Nevius family had lived in this house. It was originally built as a one-and-a-half-story farmhouse and was later modernized during the Victorian period when A. Layton Nevius married Henrietta Van Doren. From 1971 to 1978, the house served as the Bedminster Township Library. (Clarence Dillon Library.)

This photograph of the Bedminster Dutch Reformed Church parsonage was taken in 1900. Known as "Shady Grove Farm," the house was later purchased by Dr. Beekman and expanded in 1905. (E. Van Doren.)

Charlie Wikoff operated the stagecoach between Peapack and Somerville. This photograph was taken about 1910. (Somerset County Library.)

About 1895, Dr. John B. Beekman took this picture of the Bedminster Reformed Church parsonage. Miss Mary McNair is shown on the steps. Domine James McNair is at the left with his team and buggy. He taught a preparatory school for boys in this house. (Clarence Dillon Library.)

This is the same house as in the above photograph. Dr. Beekman purchased the house in 1902, and added a second story and a full attic. This photograph was taken in 1903. The house remained in the Beekman family until the death of Dr. Beekman's son Henry in 1983 at the age of 88. (Clarence Dillon Library.)

This photograph of the Bedminster Reformed Church was taken about 1905. The structure replaced the one that was located by the cemetery on Route 202/206. (Branchburg Historical Society.)

The interior of the Bedminster Reformed church is shown here in 1908 on the 150th anniversary of its founding. (Rutgers Special Collection.)

Members of Bedminster Reformed Church gathered on Washington's Birthday in 1914. Listed from left to right are the following: (front row) Betty McLaughlin, Martha Flomerfelt, Martha McLaughlin, May Dowling, and Mary Howard; (second row) Mildred Townley, Franklin Potter, Mr. Bockhoven, Mrs. Charles Barker, Mrs. Joseph Layton, and Eleanor Nevius; (third row) Mrs. Loretta Plotts, Mrs. A. Layton Nevius, Effie Beekman, Mrs. George Potter, Mrs. David Reinhart, Mrs. John McLaughlin, Mrs. Ellis Dow, the Reverend Charles G. Mallery (pastor from 1914 to 1919), Mrs. Mallery, Mrs. Charles High Rogers, Mrs. Bertha Lane, and A. Layton Nevius; (fourth row) Ted Stratton, Joseph Layton, Mrs. Grace Sueter, Mr. and Mrs. Rod Oakes, Mrs. P.D. Lane, Mrs. Ella Gutleber, Mabel Logan, and Mrs. Harriet Wyckoff; (back row) John McLaughlin, Blackwell Mallery, Vernon Hall, Charles Mallery, Richard Mallery, Chauncey Oakes, Ken Paulson, Mrs. Mark Osborne, Gret Van Arsdale, Marion Elmer, Mary Frost, Eleanor Stratton, Mildred Pantley, Marion Rice, and Mildred Harsell. George L. Frost took this photograph.

This photograph of the Layton funeral home was taken in 1910. (Somerset County Historical Society.)

This photograph of Mellick's Old Stone House was taken about 1889. The house was built in 1751 by Johannes Moelich, and was made famous by Andrew Mellick Jr.'s book *Story of an Old Farm, Life in New Jersey in the 18th Century*. (Rutgers Library.)

Here is another view of the Old Stone House, taken in the 1930s after the upstairs had been expanded. (Rutgers Library.)

Three

LAMINGTON

This bird's-eye view of Lamington was taken looking west from Cowperthwaite Road. The steps to the black cemetery and gravestones may be seen at the left. (E. Van Doren.)

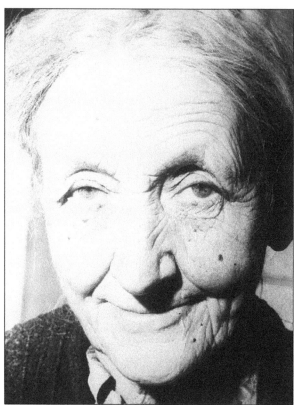

Miss Anna Sutphen of Lamington, photographed here in 1965 at about 80 years of age, remembered how the Lamington Presbyterian Church was formerly by the cemetery. It was put on huge wheels and rolled very slowly across the road to its present location. The move took a matter of months, during which time the congregation would climb up in it on Sunday and hold its worship service as usual. (Rutgers Special Collection.)

George Anthony built the Lamington general store in 1895 on the site of a previous store. In 1984, Peter and Anne Brookes bought the then-vacant store and painstakingly restored it. (E. Van Doren.)

The Lamington Presbyterian Church is pictured here after its move to the present site. The church was organized, and the first pastor called, in 1740. That year the congregation worshiped in Hezekiah Eyck's barn while the first church building was erected. The cornerstone for the present church was laid on April 3, 1826. (Branchburg Historical Society.)

The Lamington Presbyterian Church and Parsonage were photographed here about 1906. The Reverend James McCrea was the first pastor. The brutal murder of his daughter Jane by Native Americans in the service of the British during the Revolution helped to turn people against the British, and contributed to the defeat of Burgoyne at Saratoga. (E. Van Doren.)

45

The Van Nest homestead, located on a hill above the Lamington church, later became part of Hamilton farms, owned by Mr. James Cox Brady. This picture was taken about 1901. (E. Van Doren.)

This is how the corner of Lamington Road and Black River Road looked in 1965. (Rutgers Special Collection.)

Four

BURNT MILLS

In 1726 George Willocks, an East Jersey Proprietor, sold this site to Daniel Axtell, son of the regicide of the same name. His father had been commander of the guard in Westminster Hall during the trial of King Charles I. The King was convicted and beheaded. Many years later, when the King's son, Charles II, was restored to the throne, Axtell and the other regicides were themselves condemned to death. Axtell's son Daniel fled to the colonies, where he became a wealthy merchant. Daniel's son William built the first mill here. In 1754, he advertised in the *New York Gazette*: "A Compleat (sic) Mill, the house 60 by 40 feet with two Pairs of Stones, and a Room for a Third, or Convenience for a Fulling Mill under the same Roof, either of which will be erected at the expense of the Owner, situate in the County of Somerset . . . near the North Branch of the Rariton River, on a large Stream . . ." The mill was rented and later purchased by Andrew Leake, who named the location Bromley and also operated a general store here. His mill supplied flower to Washington's victorious army camped at Pluckemin following the Battle of Princeton in January 1777. Later that year, when he heard that a British foraging party was headed his way, Leake dumped all his flour and grain in the river to prevent them from capturing it. In reprisal, the British burned the mill and gave the village a new name. (Branchburg Historical Society.)

The mill was rebuilt after the Civil War. This photograph was taken between 1903 and 1909. Mr. Erdley, the miller, and his wife, Anna, are standing in the doorway. A sideshot mill, it stood on the south side of the Lamington River, just to the east of the present bridge. The mill was torn down in 1928. (Clarence Dillon Library.)

This is the 18th-century house of the miller at Burnt Mills. (Branchburg Historic Preservation Commission.)

This is a view of the mill dam at Burnt Mills, on the Lamington River, taken during the summer of 1902. Some sections of the dam still remain. (E. Van Doren.)

Here is the bridge over the Lamington River that was replaced by the present structure. (E. Van Doren.)

The Burnt Mills schoolhouse was brought from Pluckemin on rollers pulled by horses. The photographer, Edythe Van Doren, had been the teacher here, but at the time that this photograph was taken by Doren about 1904, Miss Fritts was the teacher. (E. Van Doren.)

Here is Miss Fritts and the class of about 1906. (E. Van Doren.)

This is the schoolhouse as it looks today. At first it was located closer to the river, but it was later moved to its present site due to flooding. Today it is a private residence. (Branchburg Historical Society.)

"Strawberry Fields" is the name of this beautiful vernacular Greek Revival house. What you see dates from the first half of the 19th century, but the core of the structure is a house that was built in the 1770s. (Branchburg Historic Preservation Commission.)

Here Miss Fritts, the schoolteacher, reads poetry to Ella Lane (cousin of the photographer, Edythe Van Doren). (E. Van Doren.)

Ella Lane (left) and Miss Fritts, the schoolteacher (right), are playing cards on the porch of the Lane farmhouse. The Lane farm was near Burnt Mills. (E. Van Doren.)

Five

POTTERSVILLE

Sering Potter, the owner of grist- and fulling mills, is recognized as the founder of the town that was originally called Potter's Mills. Sering also served as postmaster for 40 years, during which time the name of the town became Pottersville. This view of Pottersville was taken from the high ground on the Tewksbury side of town. (Rutgers Special Collection.)

The Pottersville Hotel was built in 1889 at the same time that the Rockaway Valley Railroad came to town. It was built by Whisky Hank (Henry) Fleming. He later sold the property to his son-in-law, Ellis Sutton. (Somerset County Historical Society.)

This is a view of the Sutton Hotel showing the barns that belong to the property. (Somerset County Historical Society.)

On August 12, 1865, a meeting was held in the local schoolhouse for the purpose of organizing a church. Sering Potter was elected chairman, and his son Jonathan became secretary. Those present voted as to which denomination to choose. Dutch Reformed was selected. The cornerstone was laid May 22, 1866, and the sanctuary was dedicated on December 26 of the same year. (Branchburg Historical Society.)

Dutch Reformed Church, Pottersville, N. J.

The Pottersville School still stands next to the firehouse. (Clarence Dillon Library.)

This was the Pottersville Store in 1894. Today it is a branch of the Peapack Gladstone Bank. (Somerset County Historical Society.)

An old up-and-down saw can be seen on the left in the foreground of this picture of the Pottersville Mill Dam taken in 1902. (E. Van Doren.)

This is the Basket Factory at Pottersville as it appeared about the turn of the century. (E. Van Doren.)

This is a view of the Pottersville Foundry, which is located in the Tewksbury part of town. (Somerset County Historical Society.)

This picture of the Pottersville Foundry shows the blacksmith shop and a house. All have been demolished. (Somerset County Historical Society.)

This is the Wortman Mill in Pottersville about 1900. (Clarence Dillon Library.)

58

This buckwheat flour sack was used at the Hildebrant Flour Mill at Pottersville. (Clarence Dillon Library.)

The Hildebrant Mill was demolished in 1969. (Clarence Dillon Library.)

Rockaway Valley Railway—June 28, 1897.

Trains. North.		Stations.	Trains. South.	
A. M.	P. M.	LEAVE. ARR.	A. M.	P. M.
5.30	1.50	Whitehouse,	11.00	7 00
F	1.56	Sweeney,	10.55	F
5.50	2.10	New Germantown,	10.45	6.45
F	2.15	Sutton,	10.35	F
6.10	2.30	Pottersville,	10.25	6.28
6.25	2.45	Peapack (Gladstone),	10.05	6.15
6.50	3 10	Ralston,	9.45	6.00
7.00	3.15	Mendham,	9.35	5.55
7.05	3.20	Pitney,	9.30	5.50
7.10	3.30	Brookside,	9.20	5.45
7.30	3.55	Watnong,	9.00	5.30
7.50	4.10	Morristown,	8.45	5.10
7.55	4.30	ARR. D.L.&W. Station, Lv.	8.40	5.05

Trains run daily except Sundays.   F Stop on flag only.

J. N. PIDCOCK, JR., SUPT.   FRANK PIDCOCK, AGT.

This timetable for the Rockaway Valley Railway shows that in 1897 there were two round trips a day between Whitehouse and Morristown. (T. Leonard Hill.)

The *P.W. Melick* was the first locomotive on the Rockaway Valley Railroad, affectionately called the Rockabye Baby Railroad. (T. Leonard Hill.)

There was a single siding at Pottersville. Here the train is picking up milk cans. Sometimes carloads of grain were shipped to Wortman's gristmill. This photograph was taken after the main passenger station burned in 1906. (T. Leonard Hill.)

Rockaway Valley Railroad's locomotive number three was named *The Rachel*. Here it is at Pottersville station about 1891. (T. Leonard Hill.)

Here is number three again. *The Rachel* was called the pride and joy of the Rockaway Valley Railroad. This photograph was taken about 1890. (T. Leonard Hill.)

This modified "Tin Lizzy" was used by the work crew to maintain the right-of-way about 1917. (T. Leonard Hill.)

Six

ALL AROUND THE TOWN

This photograph of the Todd family, posing in a field of wildflowers, was taken about 1890.
(James S. Jones.)

"Willowhurst" was the name given to the 95-acre farm on Burnt Mills Road, purchased by Ernest and Abby Lane from Phillip P. Van Arsdale in 1882. This was the home where Edythe Lane Van Doren, the photographer, grew up. It was later sold to Frederic and Esther Crego, professional ballroom dancers from New York City. The property was purchased by John Kean in 1963. (E. Van Doren.)

Entitled "Ma & Pa," this is a photograph of Ernest Erastus Lane (1852–1934) and his wife, Abby (Waldron) Lane (1856–1939), mother and father of the photographer, Edythe (Lane) Van Doren. (E. Van Doren.)

Peter Philhower Van Doren, husband of the photographer, Edythe Van Doren, poses in his "rig" in the yard at Willowhurst in 1900. (E. Van Doren.)

Edythe Van Doren's Lane grandparents (seated in chairs) and uncle, Matt Lane (standing), were photographed in 1900. (E. Van Doren.)

Here is the barnyard at Willowhurst in 1900. (E. Van Doren.)

That's not a scarecrow! It's the photographer's father, Ernest Lane, husking corn in a field in 1900. (E. Van Doren.)

Ernest Lane, brandishing a knife, has just slaughtered a number of chickens and piglets in this 1900 photograph entitled "killing time." Killing time was in the fall, when animals were slaughtered and the meat preserved with salt, or by smoking, to provide food for the family during the winter. Some animals had to be killed in the fall, because there would not be enough feed to get them all through the winter. (E. Van Doren.)

Ernest Lane is shown here on his binder around August 1900. A binder was the ancestor of the reaper/bailer. A binder cut wheat or oats and tied it with string in little round bundles. (E. Van Doren.)

Aunt Ann's house was called "The Homestead." Note the well in the right foreground. A pivot-pole was used to offset the weight of the water bucket. A person would pull down on the rope to lower the bucket into the water, and then the weight of the pole would pull the full bucket back up. (E. Van Doren.)

This peddler's rig, owned by Mr. Elliot, meandered from farm to farm, loaded with essentials and notions. (E. Van Doren.)

Mr. Welsh is shown here seated in a "gig" behind his beautiful black Morgan horse in 1902. A gig was a two-wheeled vehicle used for personal transportation. (E. Van Doren.)

The Welsh farmhouse was taken down about 1927, when Mr. and Mrs. Rivington Pyne purchased the farm to build their great estate, "Shale" (see p. 122). (E. Van Doren.)

This mill at Vliettown on the Lamington River was taken down in 1927. The property currently belongs to James C. Brady. The photograph was taken about 1900. (E. Van Doren.)

There was a siding on the Rockaway Valley Railroad in front of the Durling Creamery in Vliettown, from which a carload of milk was shipped daily. Durling Farms is now the parent company of Quick Check. (T. Leonard Hill.)

The lady on the left is Mrs. Harrie G. Pidcock. With her are her mother, Martha Sargeant Gray Waldron, and her daughter Gladys. Both of the ladies are dressed in widow's weeds. In 1900, when this picture was taken, thirty-three-year-old Mrs. Pidcock was already the widow of United States Congressman Pidcock, who died in 1899. Her stepson, James N. Pidcock, was the first president and principal owner of the Rockaway Valley Railroad. The Pidcock farm is now part of the Fiddler's Elbow golf course. (E. Van Doren.)

On a summer afternoon in 1900, the photographer's friend, Sue, poses on a split-rail fence along the road to Kline's Mill. (E. Van Doren.)

This house, built by Abraham Van Arsdale in the early 1800s, was later owned by Jacob Kline, who operated a grist and sawmill on the site. Kline was also a colonel in the militia, a member of the New Jersey Legislature, president of a bank in Trenton, and the New Jersey State Treasurer. After his death, his son sold the house and mills in 1899 to Hamilton Fish Kean, one of the owners of the Elizabethtown Water Company. The Kean family purchased a number of mills in the Raritan watershed to acquire the water diversion rights that went with them. Kean became an senator from 1925 to 1935, and was the grandfather of Gov. Thomas Kean. The house was rented at the turn of the century to Horace J. Subers, the president of the Somerville Water Company. (E. Van Doren.)

The photographer, Edythe Van Doren, is on the right, and her friend Sue is on the left in this photograph, taken in 1900. The Kline's Mill bridge can be seen in the background. (E. Van Doren.)

This photograph depicts Kline's Mill, the millrace, and the miller's cottage. The foundation stones for the mill came from the old St. Paul's stone Lutheran church in Pluckemin, which was taken down in 1821. This is perhaps the last example of an up-and-down sawmill in New Jersey. The equipment is still in place, and the dams and spillways have been maintained. The property is owned by the Kean family. (E. Van Doren.)

This is the bridge over the North Branch of the Raritan River at Kline's Mills as it appeared in 1904. (E. Van Doren.)

This house on Kline's Mills Road, belonging to Mrs. Van Arsdale at the turn of the century, was built about 1840 by Tunis Vanderveer Van Arsdale. John Kean, grandson of Sen. Hamilton Fish Kean and cousin of Gov. Thomas Kean, purchased the house in 1955. (E. Van Doren.)

"Elm Crest," located on Burnt Mills Road, was built by the Vroom family, and was later owned by the McMurtry family. (E. Van Doren.)

Nell Adah poses in 1902 with her horse. (E. Van Doren.)

This photograph, taken about 1901, is simply titled "Chick and Horse." (E. Van Doren.)

The photographer had many creative ideas for postcards, which were used extensively at the turn of the century to send messages in the days before the telephone. This is the photographer, Edythe Van Doren, on the left, and Daisy Demond on the right. (E. Van Doren.)

This 1900 photograph called "Hands and Feet" was taken on the porch of the photographer's Pluckemin home. The photographer is third from the right. (E. Van Doren.)

Even at the turn of the century, people liked to clown around for the camera. Three of these ladies are really gentlemen, and one even has a mustache. Remember that all these pictures were time exposures, so everyone had to remain perfectly still. Notice how three of them are supporting their heads with their hands. The exposure was over one minute. (E. Van Doren.)

In 1900, people did not wear casual clothes, even to a picnic. (E. Van Doren.)

To say "I love you" or "I miss you" were frequent reasons to send postcards at the turn of the century, so Edythe Van Doren had several cards with love themes. (E. Van Doren.)

In this 1902 postcard, Edythe Van Doren is the lady, and her sister Maude is posing as the gentleman. (E. Van Doren.)

In this little love nest is Edythe Van Doren on the right, and her sister Maude, posing as a man, on the left. (E. Van Doren.)

This portrait is of Daisy and Lester Demond in 1900. (E. Van Doren.)

Francis K. Stevens was the second president of the Peapack Gladstone Bank, serving from 1934 to 1945. He lived at "Stone House Farm" on Ballentine Road, near where the United States Equestrian Team is today. (James S. Jones.)

Jack Wilmerding was the honorary secretary of the Essex Hunt Club. The logo for the Peapack Gladstone Bank was taken from this picture. (James S. Jones.)

Seven

THE LANDED GENTRY

In the late 1800s, the Bernardsville Mountain Colony became the fashionable place for very wealthy New Yorkers to establish their country estates. When there was no land left in Bernardsville, the next generation located in Far Hills and Peapack-Gladstone. The third generation bought up all the farmland in Bedminster. In 1892, Charles Pfizer bought 200 acres of land west of Gladstone for his Essex Hounds. The hounds, the hunters (the horses), and the equipment were his private property until the organization was incorporated in 1913 as a private subscription club. The club hunted the farms and estates of Bedminster, and as far away as Belle Meade in Hillsborough. Here are the Essex Foxhounds in 1913, under the supervision of George Brice, huntsman, on the Burnt Mills Road in Pluckemin. The Pluckemin School can be seen on the left. (James S. Jones.)

Clarence Dillon (left) and John Pierpont Morgan Jr. are sworn in before testifying to congress in 1933. Dillon's Polish immigrant father scrimped and saved so that his son could get a good education and a start in life. Clarence Dillon graduated from Harvard and joined William A. Read & Co. Soon he took over the company, renaming it Dillon Read & Co. (*Forbes,* July 13, 1987.)

"Dunwalke," the estate of Clarence Dillon, was constructed with bricks from Hatfield Manor in Virginia. The oversized red brick had been brought from England as ship's ballast in 1680. The Georgian-style house was designed by John Cross of Cross & Cross in New York, and was built in 1928. (Princeton University.)

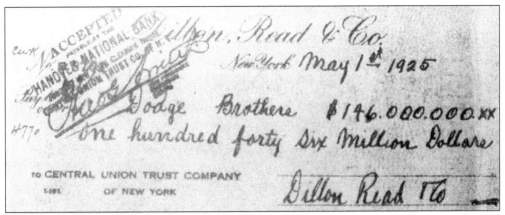

In 1921, Dillon saved the Goodyear Tire & Rubber Co. from bankruptcy by issuing high-yield bonds. In 1925, he wrote this check to buy the Dodge automobile company for $146 million, outbidding J.P. Morgan & Co. He also created the National Cash Register Company (NCR). (Dillon Read & Co.)

This is a side view of Dunwalke as viewed from the west. After the death of Clarence Dillon in 1979, the house and 126 acres were given to Princeton University to be used for a conference center and retreat. (Princeton University.)

C. Douglas Dillon, son of Clarence Dillon, served as chairman of Dillon Read & Co. from 1945 to 1953. He became under secretary of state and ambassador to France under President Eisenhower, and secretary of the treasury under Presidents Kennedy and Johnson. (*The Somerset Messenger Gazette.*)

Dunwalke East was the estate of C. Douglas Dillon. After his retirement from public service, Mr. Dillon became chairman of the New York Metropolitan Museum of Art. He owned the famous Haut Brion vineyards in France. His daughter Joan became a Duchess by marrying Prince Philippe de Mouchy. Their children are Prince Robert and Princess Charlotte de Luxembourg. (Turpin Real Estate.)

The classic Georgian home of C. Douglas Dillon was designed by Mott B. Schmidt of New York, and was built in 1936. The pediment above the front door displays pheasants carved in wood. This handsome freestanding circular stairway graces the entrance hall. (Turpin Real Estate.)

Mr. Dillon's library, paneled in light English oak, contained many rare volumes. The home has seven bedrooms, seven full bathrooms, and two half-baths. The servant's quarters contain another six bedrooms and two baths. (Turpin Real Estate.)

The entry foyer contains one of the home's eight working fireplaces. (Turpin Real Estate.)

The 22-by-33-foot living room is off the rose garden. (Turpin Real Estate.)

The fireplace in the dining room has an 18th-century marble mantelpiece. (Turpin Real Estate.)

The gardens were designed by the well-known New York landscape architects Innocenti & Vitale. (Turpin Real Estate.)

These four ladies called themselves "The Galloping Grandmas" back in 1949. They are, from left to right, Mrs. Charles (Vera) Scribner on Nearsight, Mrs. Davis (Dorothy) Pyle on Bull Run, Mrs Lester Perrin on Notable, and Mrs DeCoursey (Dorothy) Fales on Red Ember. Note that they are all riding sidesaddle. (Masters of the Essex Foxhounds.)

"Elm Pastures" was the 100-acre estate of Mrs. Lester Perrin. Mrs. Perrin was formerly the wife of State Sen. Dryden Kuser. At another time, this was the home of Millicent Fenwick at the beginning of her married life, long before becoming the beloved congresswoman. (Turpin Real Estate.)

Kenneth B. Schley, son of Grant and Elizabeth Schley, was photographed on Mendoza about 1916. Mr. Schley graduated from Yale in 1902, and soon entered the world of Wall Street. He became prominent as a stockbroker with the firm of Moore & Schley. He served as a member of the board of directors in many important firms. In October of 1941, he entertained the Duke and Duchess of Windsor at his home in Bedminster. (Kenneth B. Schley Jr.)

Mr. Schley bought the Field farm, along the Lamington River, and built this house, which is modeled after the governor's mansion at Williamsburg, Virginia. John D. Rockefeller provided the bricks, and roofing shingles (which are terra cotta, but look like cedar shakes) from the same batches as those that were being used to restore the governor's mansion. Mr. Schley served as joint master of the Essex Foxhounds with James Cox Brady. The opening meet of the Essex Foxhounds in the 1936 season was held here. (Kenneth B. Schley Jr.)

"October House," now known as "Foxwood," was purchased by William Thorn and Frances Dallett Kissel in 1918. Mr. Kissel was the son of esteemed banker Gustav Kissel, and the great-grandson of Cornelius Vanderbilt. When Cornelius Vanderbilt died in 1887, he left an estate of $105 million, which was more money than there was in the United States Treasury at the time. (Turpin Real Estate.)

Here is another view of the William Thorn Kissel estate. Mr. Kissel was a member of the Essex Hunt Club, which was just down the road. He was also the founder of the Burnt Mills Polo Club in 1930, and originally owned all the ponies and equipment. Mr. Kissel maintained a polo field on the grounds of his estate, even though the property was not perfectly level. (Turpin Real Estate.)

90

"Crossfields" was the estate of Drew Mellick, a partner in an odd lots stock-trading firm on Wall Street. It was designed by the firm of Hyde & Shepard of New York, and was built in 1931. (Turpin Real Estate.)

"The Fields" is a brick with slate roof, country house designed by Roger Bullard of New York for Mr. and Mrs. John Balfour Clark of the Clark Thread Company. It was built in 1928. In 1950, the house and 130 acres were purchased by Mr. and Mrs. G.W. Merck. (James S. Jones.)

"Hamilton Farms," the James Cox Brady estate, is shown here as it looked in 1913. The house burned in 1921, and was rebuilt on an even grander scale as a brick, Georgian-style mansion, with 64 rooms, 11 fireplaces, 2 elevators, and a chapel. Mr. Brady was a financier who was attracted to the area by his friendship with Charles Pfizer, and his association with the Essex Foxhounds. The estate, named for Mr. Brady's first wife, Elizabeth J. Hamilton, grew to be 5,000 acres in Somerset, Hunterdon, and Morris Counties. (Beneficial Corporation.)

Here are the Essex Foxhounds in front of Mr. Brady's stable in 1923. The stable was considered the most lavish in the United States. The interior has tile walls and terrazzo floors. There are 54 box stalls, each 12-feet square. There are 40 rooms in the stable, including ten sleeping rooms, an apartment for the manager, recreation rooms, and a study/trophy room over the main door with a glass floor, so that Mr. Brady could inspect his carriage before it left the building. (Beneficial Corporation.)

The Brady mansion burned again in the 1980s, and has been rebuilt by the Beneficial Corporation. (Collection of the authors.)

In the mid-1930s, James Cox Brady Jr. (left) and Kenneth B. Schley (right) were joint masters of the Essex Foxhounds. In the center is George Brice, the huntsman. (Kenneth B. Schley Jr.)

In 1916, James Cox Brady Sr. bought the entire 134-acre farm and Vliettown Mill settlement to add to Hamilton farm. Mr. Brady kept his Clydesdale and Percheron farm workhorses here. The mill was kept working to grind feed for the hundreds of animals on Hamilton farm until Mr. Brady's death in 1927. The mill was taken down in 1929. (James S. Jones.)

The "Mill House at Vliettown" was originally the 18th-century miller's house. After major alterations and additions in 1929, it became the home of Mr. Brady' son James. The public road was diverted to the former right-of-way of the Rockaway Valley Railroad, and the old road became Mr. Brady's driveway. The Mill House is now owned by Mr. and Mrs. James Cox Brady; Mr. Brady is the grandson of the original gentleman of the same name. (James S. Jones.)

This house was built by Aaron and Magdalen Longstreet about 1820. It sits on the crest of the hill overlooking Lamington. In 1925, the house and 190 acres were purchased by James Cox Brady. The house was renovated in the 1950s, and became the home of Mr. and Mrs. Ruben Richards in 1960. Mrs. Richards is a granddaughter of James Cox Brady. (James S. Jones.)

This house and farm were owned by John Honeyman from 1793 to 1822. In 1915 James Cox Brady bought it. The house now belongs to the family of Ruth Batcheller, a daughter of Mr. Brady. (James S. Jones.)

Mr. Nicholas Brady, grandson of James Cox Brady, became president and CEO of Dillon Read & Company in 1971. In 1982, Governor Kean appointed him to the Senate to finish the term of Harrison Williams, who had resigned. In 1988, President Reagan named him secretary of the treasury, and President Bush retained him in that capacity. Bush and Brady were close friends. (Somerset County Library.)

This 19th-century farmhouse and 114 acres were purchased by James Cox Brady in 1917. It would be difficult to recognize the structure today because there were major alterations and additions made to the structure in 1939 for Mr. Brady's daughter Virginia upon her marriage to John K. Cowperthwaite. In 1957 it became the home of Nicholas Brady. He named it "Dogpatch." His son now lives in the house. (Collection of the authors.)

Mr. Frederic Mosley (left) and Mr. John Winston (right) take a jump in the 1940 Pfizer Cup Race. (James S. Jones.)

The clubhouse at Fiddler's Elbow Country Club was formerly the estate of Mr. and Mrs. Frederic Mosley. Mr. Mosley was a New York investment banker. Mrs. Mosley was the sister of James Cox Brady. Today, Mr. Raymond Donovan, who served as secretary of labor under Pres. Ronald Reagan, is a partner in the ownership of the club. (Collection of the Authors.)

This colonial home, built in the 1760s, is perched on a rise overlooking the North Branch of the Raritan River. In 1950 an indoor swimming pool wing, designed by architect James S. Jones, was added by Mr. and Mrs. Heyward Cutting, who called the estate "Cutting Corner." The property was later occupied by Mr. and Mrs. Peter Kissel, who called it "River Run Farm." (Turpin Real Estate.)

"Redfield Stable" consists of an elaborate courtyard in the Federal style. It was designed and built in 1920 by William W. Cordingley, who was an architectural historian and mayor of Mendham. He also designed the main buildings at the St. John the Baptist School and Convent in that town. Miss Emily Stevens, of the Stevens family of Hoboken, owner of the estate at the time, was a breeder of fine hunters (horses). (James S. Jones.)

"Hickory Corner" was the estate of Jacqueline Mars, heiress to one-fourth of the Mars candy business. The company was founded in 1911 by her grandparents, Frank and Ethel Mars. The first big success was the Milky Way bar, suggested by her father because of his fondness for malted milk. He is also credited with developing M&Ms, after seeing candy-coated chocolate drops during the Spanish Civil War. (Turpin Real Estate.)

Built in 1915 as a country retreat, Hickory Corner is seen here from the rear. Jacqueline Mars' interest in Mars, Inc. has been estimated to be worth $3 billion, which could make her the richest woman in the world. (Turpin Real Estate.)

Designed by Henry R. Sedgewick and built between 1928 and 1932, this estate on Cowperthwaite Road was called Middlebrook by its owner, Mr. Harold Fowler. A member of the Essex Hunt Club, Mr. Fowler hosted fox hunts on many occasions. Today the property is called "Stone Bridge Farm." (Turpin Real Estate.)

The Essex Foxhounds are seen here at the Fowler's Middlebrook Farm on Thanksgiving Day in 1932. Listed from left to right, the hunters are Betty Thompson, Mrs. Charles (Vera) Scribner, Virginia Brice, Miles Valentine; George Brice (the huntsman), and Ken Schley (master of the Essex Foxhounds). (Kenneth B. Schley Jr.)

This estate adjoining Clarence Dillon's Dunwalke was owned in the early 1900s by Joseph Laroque, a partner in the New York law firm of Choate, Laroque, & Mitchell. More recently, it was owned by Mr. and Mrs. William Phillips. Mr. Phillips was a partner in Dillon Read & Company. (Turpin Real Estate.)

In 1912 this was the home of Mr. and Mrs. Archibald Alexander, parents of the Archibald Alexander who became treasurer of the state of New Jersey, and under secretary of the army, among other posts. In 1914 the estate was purchased by Mr. and Mrs. DeCoursey Fales. Mr. Fales was president of the Fulton Trust Company, and a commodore of the New York Yacht Club. (Turpin Real Estate.)

John Z. De Lorean left his job as vice president of General Motors to found the De Lorean Motor Company in Northern Ireland. Christina Ferrare was Mrs. John De Lorean at the time that the couple purchased Lamington House. (*The Somerset Messenger Gazette.*)

Lamington House is the estate of John De Lorean. When he bought this 433-acre estate in 1981, the $3.5 million price was the highest ever paid for a property in this area. (Turpin Real Estate.)

This is the entry foyer at Lamington House as it looked when it belonged to John K. Cowperthwaite Jr. He was of the third and last generation of the Cowperthwaite family to reside at the house. (Turpin Real Estate.)

Here is John K. Cowperthwaite Jr.'s study at Lamington House. Mr. Cowperthwaite's grandfather, Morgan Cowperthwaite, had started the estate with the purchase of a 142-acre farm from Robert and Estelle Smith in 1917. Morgan Cowperthwaite, an insurance broker, designed the front portico of the house, built in 1939, to resemble the one on the White House. (Turpin Real Estate.)

Florence, Mrs. Frederick W. Jones Jr., is standing in front of her home, "Little Lane Lodge," in 1910. Mr. and Mrs. Jones purchased the house and 40 acres in 1902. They made several additions and alterations to the house. They had moved to the area to hunt with Charles Pfizer's Essex Foxhounds. Mr. Jones became the local real estate broker, and sold many city people country estates in the area. (James S. Jones.)

Mrs. Jones walks by the barn at Little Lane Lodge during the year before they bought the farm. Mr. Jones had been a member of Squadron A of the 7th New York National Guard. To gain some real horseback riding experience, instead of just riding in a ring inside a city building, he joined Charles Pfizer to hunt foxes on weekends. (James S. Jones.)

Mrs. Florence Jones poses on Caliban in front of the stable at Little Lane Lodge in 1908. Notice that she is riding sidesaddle. (James S. Jones.)

Mr. Frederick W. Jones Jr. is seen here astride his great hunter, Caliban. Caliban was foaled in 1905 and was reserve champion in 1912 and 1913. Mr. Jones rode him with the Essex Foxhounds for 20 consecutive years until 1929. (James S. Jones.)

Here is Mr. James S. Jones on a "dogcart" about 1935. A dogcart was a wagon with a compartment under the seat for the transportation of hunting hounds. (James S. Jones.)

These are the barns at Little Lane Lodge as they appeared in 1913. The property was sold to Mr. and Mrs. Philip Smith in 1929. (James S. Jones.)

Once president of Abercrombie & Fitch, John H. "Jack" Ewing became state senator for Somerset County. He served in World War II as an airborne infantry officer, making combat jumps in Okinawa, Corrigedor, the Phillipines, and Dutch New Guinea. He served again during the Korean War, earning a bronze medal for valor. In 1951, he married Alison Pyne, daughter of Grafton Pyne. (*The Somerset Messenger Gazette.*)

Little Lane Lodge became the estate of Senator and Mrs. John Ewing. Extensive alterations were made for them by architect Bradley Delanty. The property now includes a private polo field, added by a subsequent owner. (Turpin Real Estate.)

In 1743, Guisbert Sutphen and his wife, Ariantje Van Pelt, came to Bedminster with a yoke of oxen and a cart on which were all their worldly possessions, including the chest of carpenter tools with which he built this house. In the 1920s the house was purchased by Mr. and Mrs. James McAlpin Pyle. Extensive alterations were made under the direction of New York architect A. Musgrave Hyde. (Turpin Real Estate.)

The center-aisle, 12-stall stable was moved to this site from "McAlpin Corner" on Jockey Hollow Road in Morris County. After Mr. Pyle's death, his widow married Dr. Augustus Knight, the medical director of Metropolitan Life Insurance Company. After World War II, the estate was owned by Mr. and Mrs. Nelson Slater. Mrs. Slater was master of the Essex Foxhounds. (Turpin Real Estate.)

"Merriewold West" was the name given to this estate by its former owner, Mary Lea Johnson D'Arc. Mrs. D'Arc is the daughter of Seward Johnson, and the granddaughter of Robert Wood Johnson, the founder of Johnson & Johnson. She lived in this house during her marriage to psychiatrist Victor D'Arc. She named the estate after Merriewold, the estate of her father, across the river from the Johnson & Johnson headquarters in New Brunswick. Today the property is called "Rheinland Farm." (Turpin Real Estate.)

"Spook Hollow Farm" is the estate of Mr. William V. Griffin, who was the president of the Brady Security and Realty Company. He was also the head of the English Speaking Union, a group dedicated to the improvement of relations between the United States and Great Britain, before and during World War II. After the war, Spook Hollow played host to such notables as Field Martial Viscount Bernard Montgomery. (Turpin Real Estate.)

In 1941, Chip Wood drew this picture of Vera G. Bloodgood, Mrs. Charles Scribner, with Pottersville in the background. Mrs. Scribner was master of the Essex Foxhounds for many years. An accomplished rider, she always rode (and jumped) sidesaddle. (James S. Jones.)

"Merry Brook Farm" was constructed by Mr. and Mrs. Charles Scribner in 1926. This classic Georgian mansion was designed by architect A. Musgrave Hyde of New York. The house was later owned by Mr. and Mrs. H.O.H. Frelinghuysen. (Turpin Real Estate.)

The entry foyer is graced by
this spectacular flying staircase.
(Turpin Real Estate.)

Charles Scribner was the president of the publishing firm of Scribner & Sons. He was a personal
friend of Ernest Hemingway, and published all of his works. This is the library at the Scribner
estate. (Turpin Real Estate.)

Mrs. Screven Lorillard makes a jump in perfect form. Mrs. Lorillard is a member of the Essex Foxhounds. Notice that the horse's hair has been clipped everywhere except for his legs (to protect him from brambles) giving him the appearance of wearing stockings. (Mrs. Screven Lorillard.)

Mr. Screven Lorillard is seen here at an event of the Essex Foxhounds during the 1940s. Mr. Lorillard was the great-grandson of Pierre Lorillard, the founder of the P. Lorillard Tobacco Company. (Masters of the Essex Foxhounds.)

The Lorillard estate was originally designed by Montague Flagg for Mr. and Mrs. R. Stuyvesant Pierrepont and built in 1914. They called it "Peapacton." The beautiful courtyard stable was used temporarily as a convalescent home for veterans of World War I. Mr. Screven and Mrs. Alice Whitney Lorillard purchased the property after World War II, calling it "Bindon Farm." (Mrs. Screven Lorillard.)

At the running of the Essex Foxhounds, Mrs. Lorillard, fourth from the right, surveys the field. (Mrs. Screven Lorillard.)

Mr. John Pierrepont is a direct descendant of Sir Robert de Pierrepont, who was a companion-in-arms of William the Conqueror in 1066; the Reverend James Pierrepont, one of the founders of Yale University; and John Jay, one of the chief justices of the United States Supreme Court. He is related to J. Pierpont Morgan, and the Earl of Manvers. (Masters of the Essex Foxhounds.)

Originally an 18th-century farmhouse belonging to Guisbert Sutphen and his line, the house and lands were purchased by R. Stuyvesant Pierrepont before World War I and used as a home for his tenant farmer. During the 1930s and 1940s, the house was rented to a number of people including Mr. and Mrs. Prentice Talmage. In 1951, architect James S. Jones made extensive alterations and additions for Mr. and Mrs. John Pierrepont. (Turpin Real Estate.)

The living room at Peapacton is spacious and artfully decorated. (Turpin Real Estate.)

Here is Mr. and Mrs. John Pierrepont's dining room with the table set for eight. (Turpin Real Estate.)

There are several fireplaces at Peapacton. A beautifully embroidered stool invites you to warm yourself by the fire. (Turpin Real Estate.)

This is the hall at Peapacton during the tenure of the Pierrepont family. Today the home is owned by Mr. Michael Price, whose stockbrokerage firm was responsible for the merger of the Chase Manhattan and Chemical Banks. (Turpin Real Estate.)

From left to right, this is James S. Jones, Francis Johnson, and David Pyle at the Far Hills Fair Grounds. Mr. Jones' father, Frederick W. Jones, owned Red Barns (shown below) in 1929. Mr. Francis Johnson was the owner at another time. Mr. Pyle lived up the street at Timberfields, where Malcolm Forbes would later reside. (James S. Jones.)

The 18th-century farmhouse and estate named "Red Barns" was owned by Mr. and Mrs. Richard V.N. Gambrill prior to moving to Vernon Manor in Peapack in 1927. To the rear of the handsome stonewalled stable courtyard is the initial kennel of the Vernon-Somerset Beagles. (James S. Jones.)

On Columbus Day in 1912, the Essex Hounds, still owned by Mr. Charles Pfizer, met at Riverside Farm on Kline's Mill Road. At that time the farm belonged to James and Emma (Van Arsdale) Ten Eyck. The Kline's Mill bridge may be seen on the left. This estate was later to become the property of John Kean, cousin of Governor Kean. (Masters of the Essex Foxhounds.)

During the time that Mr. Pfizer owned the Essex Hounds, he owned all of the foxhounds, most of the hunters (horses), and most of the equipment seen in this photograph. All of the riders (over 50) were Mr. Pfizer's guests. Mr. Pfizer may be seen in the center on the gray. The following year, Mr. Pfizer fell into hard financial times because of the outbreak of World War I and since Pfizer's parent company was in Germany. Mr. Pfizer could no longer afford the cost of the Essex Hounds alone. A group of his friends took over for him, reorganizing the Essex Hounds on a subscription basis, and renaming them, "The Essex Foxhounds." Under this form and name the group still exists today as the most exclusive club in the area. (Masters of the Essex Foxhounds.)

Mr. John Kean is a grandson of Sen. Hamilton Fish Kean, and first cousin of Gov. Thomas Kean, who also lives in Bedminster. (Fabian Bachrach.)

"Riverside Farm" was renamed "Lindenfeld" by John Kean when he purchased the property in 1955. Eldredge Snyder, an architect from New York, made extensive alterations in 1958. (Turpin Real Estate.)

The Frelinghuysen family is one of Somerset County's oldest, having been founded by Jacobus Frelinghuysen, a Dutch Reformed minister who came to America to lead several congregations in the early 1700s. Since then, the family has boasted generals, statesmen, senators, and congressmen. This is H.O.H. Frelinghuysen. (Conway Studios Corporation.)

Once part of the Richard Todd Farm, the house and 168-acre farm were sold to Julius Miller c. 1880. It was sold to Clarence Dillon in 1932 and sold again to Ogden White c. 1935. Mr. White was a principal in the brokerage house of White, Weld, & Co. It was rebuilt after a fire in 1947. The house and 6 acres were purchased c. 1975 by Mr. and Mrs. H.O.H. Frelinghuysen, and named "River House." (Turpin Real Estate.)

Senator and Mrs. Rivington Pyne were members of the Essex Hunt Club, and are seen here participating in the 1930 fox hunt at their estate. Mrs. Pyne is riding sidesaddle. Senator Pyne was the son of Percy Pyne, and Mrs. Pyne was the daughter of C. Ledyard Blair. (Masters of the Essex Foxhounds.)

"Shale," was the estate of State Senator and Mrs. Rivington Pyne. Senator Pyne served as a private secretary to American Ambassador James W. Gerard in Berlin from 1914 until the outbreak of World War I. During the war he served in the Army Air Corps. (Turpin Real Estate.)

While in residence here, H. Rivington Pyne was elected to the New Jersey Assembly and the state senate. He also served as chairman of the Republican Party. Later this home belonged to John McGraw, a descendant of the founder of the McGraw-Hill publishing empire. Mr. McGraw called the estate River Run Farm. (Turpin Real Estate.)

The Essex Foxhounds are shown at the Pyne mansion in 1930. (Kenneth B. Schley Jr.)

Shale was built in 1927 on a 125-acre farm. The architect was Delano and Aldrich of New York. Mr. William Adams Delano, a cousin of Franklin Delano Roosevelt, was an extremely prominent architect at the time. This is the morning room. (Turpin Real Estate.)

This is the dining room at Shale. (Turpin Real Estate.)

Shale boasts a spacious library. (Turpin Real Estate.)

This is one of the bedrooms at Shale. (Turpin Real Estate.)

Perhaps best known for his flamboyant lifestyle, Malcolm Forbes set six world records in hot air ballooning. He owned a sumptuous yacht named the *Highlander* and a Bowing 747 named the *Capitalist Tool*. In addition to his Bedminster estate he owned a 20,000-acre ranch in Montana; the 260-square-mile Trinchera Ranch in Colorado; the Chateau de Balleroy in Normandy; the Palis Mendoub in Tangiers, Morocco; and one of the Fiji Islands. Elizabeth Taylor was on his arm at his 70th birthday bash in Tangiers, which hosted almost one thousand guests, including the King of Morocco, and continued non-stop for three days. (*The Somerset Messenger Gazette.*)

Malcolm Forbes brought his family to Bedminster in 1947. He spent six years as a Republican state senator in the 1950s, but was defeated in a bid for governor in 1957. "Timberfield" was the estate of Malcolm Forbes. The c. 1800 structure was extensively renovated and expanded by architect A. Musgrave Hyde for the previous owners, Mr. and Mrs. David McAlpin Pyle. (James S. Jones.)

Upon the death of his father, Malcolm S. (Steve) Forbes Jr. (right) became the head of the Forbes publishing empire. When this photograph was taken, Barbara Bush was first lady, and Tom Kean was governor. Governor Kean also lives in Bedminster, on an estate between the Bradys and the Dillons. (*The Somerset Messenger Gazette.*)

"Southdown" is the estate of Steve and Sabina (Beekman) Forbes and their five daughters, Sabina, Roberta, Catherine, Moira, and Elizabeth. Dating from about 1800, the house was greatly altered and enlarged in 1940 under the direction of architect A. Musgrave Hyde. Mr. Forbes has added substantially to his land holdings, which now extend to the Raritan River and encompass the former Burnt Mills Polo Club field. (Turpin Real Estate.)

Here is Frederick W. Clucas, with his White Oaks Foot Beagles, about 1925. Mr. Clucas was the owner of the stock brokerage firm of F.W. Clucas. He was James Cox Brady's personal stockbroker. He was also the grandfather of world-renowned mezzo-soprano opera star Frederica von Stade ("Flicka"), who grew up in Oldwick. (James S. Jones.)

In 1915 a house that had been a colonial stagecoach stop on Lamington Road was moved to this site and enlarged to become "White Oaks Farm," the seat of the master of the White Oaks Foot Beagles. Mr. Clucas was also interested in ships and sailing. His study was constructed of arched and bolted oak that was originally a cabin aboard an old sailing vessel. (Turpin Real Estate.)

128

Lightning Source UK Ltd.
Milton Keynes UK
UKHW031919160922
409000UK00004B/100